PHIL BOWEN
Cuckoo Rock

PHIL BOWEN was born in Liverpool in 1949 where he
taught drama until 1979. He has worked as a full-time
writer, performer and teacher since 1994, visiting over
five hundred schools as a writer-in-education in more
than thirty counties. Work from his first full collection
Variety's Hammer was selected for *The Forward Anthol-
ogy* of 1998. His biography of the Mersey Poets *A
Gallery to Play to* has recently been updated and repub-
lished by Liverpool University Press, and in April 2009,
Salt published *Nowhere's Far: New & Selected poems
1990–2008*. This is his first book for children.

Also by Phil Bowen

PHIL BOWEN

Cuckoo Rock

Illustrated by Fred James

CHILDREN'S POETRY LIBRARY
No. 3

SALT

LONDON

PUBLISHED BY SALT PUBLISHING
14a High Street, Fulbourn,
Cambridge CB21 5DH United Kingdom

© Phil Bowen, 2010
Illustrations © Fred James, 2010

The right of Phil Bowen to be identified as the
editor of this work has been asserted by him in accordance
with Section 77 of the Copyright, Designs and Patents Act 1988.

First published 2010

Printed in the UK by the MPG Books Group

Typeset in Oneleigh 11 / 14

ISBN 978 1 84471 757 6 paperback

1 3 5 7 9 8 6 4 2

in memory of Adrian Mitchell
and special thanks and gratitude to the following
eleven schools in which I have worked regularly
as a visiting poet since 1995:

Trythall CP School, SW Cornwall

Bickleigh C of E School, Devon
Instow CP School, North Devon
Two Moors CP School, Tiverton, Devon

St Thomas CP School, Swansea
Mayals CP School, Swansea
Pontilliw CP School, Swansea
Dolafon CP School, Llanwrtyd Wells, Powys
Laugharne CP School, Carmarthenshire

Lowther CP School, Barnes, London SW13

St Silas C of E School, Dingle, Liverpool

CONTENTS

ACKNOWLEDGEMENTS

'Cuckoo Rock', 'Magical Valley' and much of the landscape for the book arose from a residency with Aunehead Arts called 'Granite Shadows' on Dartmoor in 2006. Some of the fish poems came from an earlier collaborative arts project — 'Electric Fish' — co-ordinated by Creative Partnerships and KEAP in Cornwall 2002.

Special thanks to Carol Ann Duffy, for stiffening my resolve when I didn't think I could write well for a younger age group.

CUCKOO ROCK

Crossing over the Clapper Bridge,
Heading for Cuckoo Rock
Peering inside potato caves,
Woodpeckers taking stock

Of what's been left in the Blowing House
Left of Tinner's Mill
Where singing nettles and bracken
Sing to the magpie still:

Sometimes you may see them
Sometimes you may not
Keep your eyes wide open
They're difficult to spot

Then call to the crow and the jayfly
Yaffle at the Yaffling Tree,
Follow the swallow tomorrow
Bring back tomorrow to me

As today and the rest of the week
Lie there in granite and heather
Lie and remain in the bluebell gorse
Lie there in all kinds of weather:

And sometimes you may see it
Sometimes you may not
Keep your eyes wide open
It's difficult to spot

As hard to find as the finger sign
On the hand of the talking clock,
Crossing over the Clapper Bridge
Heading for Cuckoo Rock.

MAGICAL VALLEY

The pipeline lies in the pathway,
The pathway lies in the place
Of Mother-Rock and Water-Rock:
    Wipe that mess off your face!

The raven crows to the blackbird,
The blackbird starts to shiver
In naval-weed and buttonwort:
    Keep your eye on the river!

Where Water-Rock and Mother-Rock
Rock the water to sleep
Now the ivy's gone and the ferns have gone:
    If it wasn't deer it was sheep!

And after that, the darkness,
Darkness inside the clay
And whatever it was the crystal saw:
    Put all of that away!

Says Mother-Rock to Water-Rock
From rock to rock to rock:
    Then throw away the crystal,
    Put eyes in the weathercock!

Where the pipeline lying in the pathway
Is the pathway's side of the alley —
And a nesting box is a nesting box
Here in Magical Valley.

HEAVEN KNOWS

Is it a crow or a jayfly?
A snake on the Yaffling Tree?
Is it Sting of the Singing Nettles
Or Fern who can sting like a bee?

Is it Ivy over from Ivybridge
With her dancing songs of Spring?
Is it the most raving of raving ravens
Raving about everything?

Is it something found in the Blowing House,
An emerald on a magic dish?
Is it naval-weed or buttonwort —
The flash of an electric fish?

Is it the reason for bits of truth?
Or only the reason that lies?
No — it is simply the reason
For the whole of the earth and the skies.

THIS IS THE WAY

This is the way
And here is the gate
You can come all the way
But you'll have to wait

For excitement
Wait for the thrill
Of crossing that bridge
To Tinner's Mill

Wait for what ticks
Then for the tock
These amazing tricks
Around Cuckoo Rock

Wait for the fun
All the wild romance —
When the Cuckoo Man comes
When he starts to dance

When he does whatever
And whatever that seems
Then wait for the girl
Who gathers dreams

So stay in the moonlight
Stay for a wish
Wait by the pond
For electric fish

Then stand on the hill
High on the ridge
Call out to Ivy
From Ivybridge

And listen to the mermaid —
The song she sings
Listen to jingling
Jangling things

Listen in a place
Where you hear the most
Then listen in the darkness
Listen for a ghost

Listen to the 'toot-toot!'
Listen to the drum —
As magical music
Is bound to come

From sounds in the valley
Sounds on the wing
And those singing nettles —
Fern and Sting

FERN AND STING

Fern and Sting

Fern and Sting

We're the Singing Nettles

Fern and Sting

We burn and sing

Burn and sing

We're the Singing Nettles

Fern and Sting

Sting and Fern

Sting and Fern

So much to learn

With Sting and Fern

Sting and Fern

We sing and burn

We're the Singing Nettles

Sting and Fern

WAYS AND WAYS
After George Mackay Brown

The way to Cuckoo Rock
is earth, wishes, bluebell gorse.

The way to the Potato Caves
is salt and loam.

We call the way to Ivybridge,
the Pipeline Way.

Every way to Moonlight
is nineteen kinds of a way.

Mister Cuckoo Man's feet
have beaten a wayside track to Cuckootown.

And the way from the Blowing House
is bracken, moss, bridges, another wish.

Crows and jayflies
have the whole huge sky as a way.

NINE BIRDS

The swallow followed
The rook rooked
The magpie saw through it all

The crow crowed
The raven raved
The magpie saw through it all

The woodpecker pecked
The blackbird wrecked
The magpie saw through it all

The jayfly flew
Through the bluebird's blue
As the magpie saw through it all

The clouds spread
As the sky turned red
And the magpie saw through it all

MAGPIE FINDS

Monday, the magpie found a wish
from an electric fish.
He gave it back to the river as a thought.

Tuesday, a piece of rock from a boulder.
Next Spring
it could become a door — a way in.

Wednesday, a nesting box.
He put his beak in it,
the rim, warm with moss and flowers.

Thursday, he got nothing —
an old boot
left by a shaking tree.

Friday he happened
on a raven's skull,
earth spilling out of it.

Saturday, petals for a dream.
Tinner's Mill
was wrecked around here, someone said.

Sunday, he ended up
on the hollow face of the hill.
What are clouds? Floating fog. Cotton wool.

THE YAFFLING TREE

There's birds and birds

In the Yaffling Tree

All kinds of words

In the Yaffling Tree

There's crows and crows

In the Yaffling Tree

It kind of grows —

The Yaffling Tree

Its branches spread —

The Yaffling Tree

From the hands to the head

Of the Yaffling Tree

Last year is dead

Says The Yaffling Tree

It's in its bed

Says the Yaffling Tree

So think again

Says the Yaffling Tree

I said again

Says the Yaffling Tree

So count to ten

Says the Yaffling Tree

Amen amen

Says the Yaffling Tree

TICKING SONATA

a charabanc   the song we sang   a scent of petals

a wishing well   kiss and tell   those singing nettles

the Yaffling Tree   the moonlit sea   the magpie's knack

a talking clock   tick-tock tick-tock   a chalk stack

the race we ran   the Cuckoo Man   the Cuckoo's back

a cuckoo clock at Cuckoo Rock

tick-tock ticktock

FORCES

The loudest crash of thunder
    The pounding of the waves
That distant distant drumming
    Echoing in caves

As footsteps on the Clapper Bridge
    Land on a snapping branch
And an order of storm from the demons
    Forces an avalanche

Of rocks to rumble through valleys
    Over rocks and rocks and rocks
Flatten potato caves into alleys
    Take time away from the clocks

Where the blackbird, crow and the raven
    Guard the nesting-box,
Then sing to the rook in its haven
    In a force so fierce it shocks!

OGRE BOULDER

Mist in the mountains
Getting colder

All around
The Ogre Boulder

Tides in the moon
Know nothing older

Than rocks and woods
Round Ogre Boulder

Crystal shapes
Are moving over

Towards the crows
Of Ogre Boulder

The crows and rooks
Of Ogre Boulder

Mist in the mountains
Getting colder

All around
The Ogre Boulder

NINETEEN MOONLIGHTS

Nineteen moonlights in the air
Nineteen moonlights over there
Nineteen moonlights — don't despair

Of summer daylight in the sky
Summer daylight riding by

On purple moors with purple vines
Past purple shores of celandines —
Blood red roses growing wild

A blood red rose for Friday's child
As nineteen moonlights reappear

Nineteen moonlights shining clear
Nineteen moonlights over here
Nineteen moonlights have no fear

Of blazing heat and blazing power
Blazing down in rays that shower

Purple rain on purple days
A purple stain — a purple haze
A purple garden growing wild
A blood red rose for Friday's child.

INSIDE THE SUNSET

I see the sea inside a sunset,
See the sea inside a dove,
Red signs inside a red night
As a red light shines above,

Like a wave that rides the sunset,
A white wave that rides the past,
The world reflected in water rocks
Or whatever else will last.

I see the sea inside a sunset,
See it wash away,
Blue lines inside the red sky,
Blue signs inside the day.

OGRE ROCK

Old grumpy Ogre Rock
Is dark and weird,
He sits on the skyline
With a grump in his beard:
'I'm staying here forever,'
He said,
When he first appeared.

Dark rocky particles
Around his boulder face
As his frown sits there scowling
In his Ogre place.
'I only listen to the Queen of the Demons,'
He said.
'Just in case'.

And when things get frozen
And covered with frost,
He growls out his orders —
He summons the Lost.
'Over there!' He bellows.
As all signs get crossed.

It's one of his thunder moods.
He says: 'I'm king of all of you.
You're down there — I'm up here.'
And as long the Demons claim him
What can we do?

OGRE AND UNDER

Ogre — the bricked-up face of the rock
Under the blue-lit tune of the sea
Ogre — the broken nose of the rock
Under the pearl-like lace of the sea
Ogre — the cannon ball of the rock
Under the burst balloon of the sea
Ogre — the armour plate of the rock
Under the coral crunch of the sea
Ogre — the crash-bang-wallop of the rock
Under the slip-slink-slide of the sea
Ogre — the poisoned sling of the rock
Under the rosemary branch of the sea
Ogre — the sucker punch of the rock
Under the wet slapped wrist of the sea
Ogre — the gloomy dog of the rock
Under the black cat's eye of the sea
Ogre — the crystal parts of the rock
Under the crystal parts of the sea

THE SEVENTH MOONLIGHT

Seven moonlights shining bright

Seven moonlights all in sight

   Of other moonlights.

The strangest sounds in the Mill's dark yard

Clattering, clattering, clattering hard —

All the windows locked and barred

   What's inside there?

NEARER AND NEARER

Nearer and nearer

The ground is shaking

Nearer and nearer

The trees are falling

Nearer and nearer

Mountains crumbling

Nearer and nearer

Faster! Louder!

Nearer and nearer

Faster! Faster!

Nearer and nearer

Near disaster!

WHAT THE NIGHT SAYS

The darkness says: It's night.
The stars say: Shine.
Fantasy says: It's magic.
The valley says: No it's mine.

Mystery says: It's all a puzzle.
The Dream Gatherer says: Resolved.
The brightness says: I'm fading.
The moonlight: I'm dissolved.

Memory says: Remember.
Demonica shouts out: Scream!
The awakening whispers: Sunrise.
The night says: It's all a dream.

DEMONICA

Demonica was Queen of the Demons,
She rang the midnight bell,
She once capsized a seaman's
Vessel and sent it to hell.

She shook up the ground and let it tremble,
Rocked mountains far and wide,
She hated all of those that worked hard
And had goodness on their side,

She trained the Ogre Rock to grumble
And rumble and growl in the dark,
She had a cat by the name of Woof
A cat that knew how to bark!

Three ghosts — Scary, Freaky and Spooky
Worked for Demonica now and then —
She wanted them to frighten her enemies
Especially the Night Soil Men.

THE NIGHT SOIL MEN

Night Soil Men — Night Soil Men

We'll say it again — we're the Night Soil Men

We work with soil — we work at night

We're the Night Soil Men — we get it right!

We work with spades — sometimes it's bricks

We're the Night Soil Men — we handle picks

We're inside caves and inside hovels

Digging soil — moving shovels

We work down deep — we graft and toil

When you're asleep we're shifting soil

We're the Night Soil Men — Night Soil Men

Don, Doug and Den — we're the Night Soil Men!

A CAT NAMED WOOF

I know what you're thinking
But it never did that,
It got this name because its fur had gone flat

And it looked like a cat
That wouldn't spit back,
And a bit like a cat that couldn't hit cats,

Backbone, it most definitely lacked,
So we thought we'd put some stuff in its strut
Give it some aims — straight from the gut,

Maybe some goals — even a shove
So the bark it acquired came from a love
Of the dark — just listen up above:

There are snarls in the stones
And the beams on the roof
And fire in the eyes of a cat named Woof!

INSIDE DEMONICA

Inside Demonica's teeth, the Ogre Rock's eye.
Inside the Ogre Rock's eye, Demonica's hair.
Inside Demonica's hair, the broken trees.
Inside the broken trees, Demonica's dark clouds.
Inside Demonica's dark clouds, the crumbling caves.
Inside the crumbling caves, Demonica's open mouth.
Inside Demonica's open mouth, the holeful of thorns
Inside the holeful of thorns, the eye of the storm.
Inside the eye of the storm, Demonica's tears.
Inside Demonica's tears, the blood in the rain.
Inside the blood in the rain, Demonica's gaze.
Inside Demonica's gaze, the lightning night.
Inside the lightning night, Demonica's teeth.

WHO TRASHED ME?

Who poured me away like sewage
Rusted me like caging
Rubbished me like rags

Who trashed me?

Who threw me away in the eye of a storm
Tore me and left me bleeding
Pleading

Who trashed me?

Who left me here like blood in the rain
Left me here and blamed me
Who maimed me?

Who dumped me down this holeful of thorns
Who pierced, crushed and compressed me
Suppressed me

Left me like an old boot on the dump
The slump, the clump
And the thump, thump, thump
Of being dented

Cemented

Who chucked me away like rotting wood
Who used me?

Who ripped me up and abused me

Who stabbed, cut and slashed me
Who trashed me?

Who trashed me?

THREE GHOSTS

Scary, Spooky and Freaky
Lived near Tinner's Mill
They frightened Mr Beaky
Who disappeared over the hill.

He'd long been the Mill Owner
With his bulbous nose and eyes,
Always a bit of a loner,
So it was hardly any surprise

That he moved across the valley —
Further away from Cuckoo Rock,
As the ghosts got more and more pally
With Demonica who liked them to shock!

SEE A GHOST?

I'm a ghost
I'm a ghost
No one can see me

I'm a ghost
I'm a ghost
No one believes me

I'm a ghost
I'm a ghost
Where am I going?

I'm a ghost
I'm a ghost
What am I doing?

I'll fool you and haunt you
And scare you the most

I go bump in the night
I'm a ghost I'm a ghost

NIGHT SOIL MEN AGAIN

Night Soil Men — Night Soil Men

Don, Doug and Den — we're the Night Soil Men —

We don't frighten — we don't scare

We're the Night Soil Men from Over There

We never weaken — never shirk

We're the Night Soil Men — we love our work

We do it all — we do the most

We're the Night Soil Men — never seen a ghost

Never seen a spook or ever had a fright

We're the Night Soil Men — we get it right!

Night Soil Men — Night Soil Men

We'll say it again — we're the Night Soil Men!

PLAYING STONES

Jasper

As bright as the sky's balloon
As bright as a child's new tune
As bright as red
Or as yellow as a sand dune

Or brown now as a cow
In a glade

Where Jade

Is a morning star
A gem wherever you are
A shining light
A bluish green
A sea-breaker barely seen
By the lake inside the park
But never ever as dark

Or deep as it ever seems
When moonlit midnight streams

Bring Jet

JASPER, JADE AND JET

Jasper, Jade and Jet!
The band you never forget,
Wild as the rage that fires up the stage
When it's Jasper, Jade and Jet!

Jasper gets the praise — he's the frontman!
The cut and the strut of his stuff!
And Jade in brocade on her drum-kit,
When enough's never more than enough!

Jet's guitar and the stars all around us,
The sound that rebounds in our ears
As Jasper jumps and Jade plays and thumps —
It explodes! As it soars! And it sears!

Twice as wild as the Singing Nettles —
Are you ready? Get steady! — Get set!
The three that won't leave us! — you better believe us!
When it's Jasper! And Jade! And it's Jet!

AT SPARKLING POND

Sparkling Pond is the brightest pond,
A pond that can shine and glisten,
If you ever go to Sparkling Pond
Just sit by the rocks and listen:

Hear the electric fish go 'zing!'
And the splatfish: splatter-splat!'
Hear Zenna the mermaid sing—
No prettier sound than that.

Sparkling Pond is a bubbling pond—
More refreshing than a bubbling brook,
If you ever go to Sparkling Pond
Just sit by the rocks and look

At colours from an electric fish-swirl
At Crystal Maze with its crystal air
And Zenna the fabulous fishgirl
Plaiting her long red hair.

Sparkling Pond is a musical pond,
Home to Jasper, Jade and Jet,
If you ever go to Sparkling Pond
You're bound to be very well met

By musical folk from the valley —
The twangiest 'toot toot!' and fun of the Fair
And Zenna the pride of our alley
Plaiting her long red hair.

ELECTRIC FISH

Electric Fish
Electric Fish
What do you wish?

Electric fish

In streams you glide
Yet like to hide
In lightning!

Electric Fish
Electric Fish
You like to swish
And bite things!

Are you a clock
On Electric Rock?
Do you tick
Or do you tock

*No we're not
We elect to shock
Inside things!*

SPLATFISH

Splatfish don't swish

Splatfish don't shiver

Splatfish don't splish

Splatfish don't quiver

Splatfish don't spook

No!

Splatfish don't do that!

Splatfish just look

And then go SPLAT!

Splatfish don't slink

Splatfish don't glide

Splatfish don't blink

Splatfish don't hide

Splatfish won't hook

No!

Splatfish won't do that!

Splatfish just look

And then go SPLAT!

ZENNA

There once was a mermaid called Zenna

Who coloured her hair with henna,

    She sang for sailors at night

    And others who might

Want to visit her best friend Morwenna

MORWENNA

Morwenna was a strange girl,
Some called her a gatherer of dreams,
Others said she was winter's light
Because she never seems quite what she seems.

Morwenna was a strange girl,
Much stranger than any of them knew,
But when she went away, they say,
All sorts of things came true.

The dreams she gathered got real —
Demonica began to lose powers,
The Ogre Rock started to crumble,
Rivers of perfume ran from all flowers.

IT'S A TOOT TOOT!

Drip splash
Drip splash

It's a toot toot!

Drip drip
Splash splash

It's a toot toot!

Zoom zoom
Beep beep

It's a toot toot!

Zoom zoom
Beep beep

It's a toot toot!

Choo choo
Clippety clip

It's a toot toot!

Choo choo
Clippety clip

It's a toot toot!

Choo choo
Clippety clip

It's a toot toot!

Ding ding
Twang bubble!

It's a toot toot

Ding ding
Twang bubble!

It's a toot toot!

THE CUCKOO MAN

The Cuckoo Man is coming around
    He's a bit of a lad,
    A wag and a clown,
He spins about — jumps up and down
Turns wherever he goes into Cuckootown:

    I turn wherever I go into Cuckootown!

It's Cuckoo this — and Cuckoo that
He's the Cuckoo Man — *with my Cuckoo hat!*
I'm the Cuckoo Man — with his Cuckoo hat!
How's your father? — *Alright!*

The Cuckoo Man, he's had nine lives
    He does a bit of tap,
    He ducks and dives —
Only got one arm but always thrives —
Turns wherever he goes into Cuckoo hives!

Wherever I go becomes a Cuckoo hive!

Wherever he goes becomes a Cuckoo hive!

It's toot-toot this! — and toot-toot that! —
He's the Cuckoo Man — *with my Cuckoo hat!*
I'm the Cuckoo Man — with his Cuckoo hat!

Ding-ding — twang-bubble! — *Alright!*

The Cuckoo Man is coming around
    He's a bit of a lad,
    A wag and a clown,
He spins about — jumps up and down
Turns wherever he goes into Cuckootown:

    I turn wherever I go into Cuckootown!

Wherever he goes becomes Cuckootown!!

THE DREAM GATHERER
After 'Brendon Gallagher' — Jackie Kay

e wore white — I was in black — the Dream Gatherer.
 r feet were bare — I had big boots — the Dream
    Gatherer.
 r hair was down to her waist — mine was shaved and
    cropped.
y clothes were heavy — they were worn for the weather.
 r dress was made of petals — the Dream Gatherer.

 e'd paint her toenails and wash her hair by the river
 here she'd spray herself with perfume from flowers.
 e had bracelets and anklets — dabbed herself with glitter.
 pirouette then a cartwheel. She could swing along on a
    star.
 tell everyone I knew about the Dream Gatherer.

 w she never wore shoes and her hair was past her waist
 d they'd say: 'How come you're the only one that sees
    her?'
 well, I'd say, she sparkles so much that she opens my
    eyes.
 ve watching her make footprints on the stones over the
    water.
 en one morning when reaching out to the lilies,

One morning when it was grey with rain and I was on all
      fours,
One of them says to me, 'I was talking to one of the
      Demons
Who says he knows the complete story of your Dream
      Gatherer,
Didn't you say she sprayed herself with perfume from
      flowers?
He said no perfume has ever been sprayed from flowers,

No flowers like that have ever been grown around here.'
And she was gone then, my Dream Gatherer —
Her waist length hair and all those petalled clothes,
Crouched on my haunches I thought about her every hour
And I can still sort of hold her when I want to — my Dream
      Gatherer.

IVY FROM IVYBRIDGE

I'm Ivy from Ivybridge;
I sleep with the shutters down,
On Thursdays I welcome visitors
Who come from Cuckootown —

There's Billy Bling and Bobby Bangle,
The Cuckoo Man from Cuckoo-Hive,
We do the fangle-dangle
And jump to the jitterbug-jive!

We love Jasper, Jade and Jet,
Watch them play at Sparkling Pond
And yours truly and Julie Dooley
Have formed ourselves a bond:

And it's Ivy this and Ivy that:
She sleeps with the shutters down!
'Give Billy Bling a ring — it's the funniest thing
When Bobby Bangle's back in town'

And the Cuckoo Man says his real name's Stan:
He's never been known to frown!
And yours truly and Julie Dooley
Paint red spots all over the town!

And it's Ivy this and Ivy that —
She sleeps with the shutters down!
On Thursday we're her visitors
We all come from Cuckootown!

THE BALLAD OF BOBBY BANGLE AND BILLY BLING

Bobby Bangle
　　And Billy Bling
Met on the road
　　To Ringading,

They both wore silver,
　　They both wore gold,
Some of it new —
　　Some of it old,

They wore bright colours,
　　Cut quite a dash,
They liked getting noticed —
　　Liked being flash,

They formed a team,
　　Became quite a pair —
First they were here,
　　Then they were there!

They liked to dance,
　　Liked to sing,
Bobby Bangle
　　And Billy Bling!

They shook it up,
   They shook it down!
Shook the cuckoos
   Out of Cuckootown!

They liked to jingle,
   Liked to jangle,
Billy Bling
   And Bobby Bangle!

COOL JULIE DOOLEY

Julie's strange to some of her friends,
She comes from Over There —
She's like a brand new daisy,
With her flowing, long blonde hair,

She's like a river inside its bed,
A bird without a voice,
Some say she's winter's light,
Others reckon she has no choice,

They call her the strangest-ever girl,
Some say: the miserable flower,
She stares and stares and stares
Hour upon hour upon hour,

But on Thursdays, she's in Ivybridge —
Meets the crew from Cuckootown,
She looks a perfect picture
In her latest full length gown,

Her long blonde hair full flowing
Her toenails, the brightest red,
She wears sparkling silver sandals —
A wide-brimmed hat upon her head

And when the Cuckoo Man strums his banjo,
Everyone begins to prance
But no one's quite like Julie
When she takes her shoes off to dance —

She spins round and round and around
With her swirling long blonde hair,
But when the fun is all over
She goes back to Over There.

When the fun is all over
She goes back to Over There.

THE FAMOUS FIVE

The Cuckoo Man's
    Real name was Stan
    When he began
    He banged a frying pan —
    It was in the can!

Billy Bling
    Went ding-a-ling
    Then ding-dong-ding
    Began to sing —
    It was the funniest thing!

Bobby Bangle's
    Fangle-dangle
    Went jangle-jangle
    In the mangle —
    Quite a tangle!

Julie Dooley
    Did things coolly
    At times unruly
    Never cruelly
    And truly Julie loved her jewellery.

Ivy Bridge
　　Bought a fridge
　　From Madge whose badge
　　Said 'No butter or fudge' —
　　It wouldn't budge.

The Famous Five

　　Duck and dive
　　Jump and jive
　　In Cuckoo Hive
　　To stay alive!

　　Jump and jive
　　In Cuckoo Hive
　　To stay alive!

WHAT BOBBY ASKED BILLY

Bobby Bangle said to Billy Bling:
'How can I get rid of this thing?'

What thing's that? said Bill,
'This curse!

It started bad
And now it's worse!

I got it from Demonica,'
Said Bobby Bangle,

'She didn't like my jokes
Couldn't stand my jangle!'

Billy thought hard
Then he thought again:

The only people who can help
Are the Night Soil Men,

Demonica hates them
'Cause of their working ways —

They built most of Cuckootown,
Built the Cuckoo Maze —

They build and build
While she destroys

They don't frighten easy —
They're good old boys.

'What are their names?
Bob asked Billy Bling.

'Don, Doug and Den,
Give them a ring'.

DEMONICA HATED IT ALL

The potato caves
Around Cuckoo Rock
Demonica hated them all

Those sunlit waves
On the talking clock
Demonica hated them all

The colour of cherries
The taste of plums
Demonica hated them all

Fresh ripe red berries
Those distant drums
Demonica hated them all

The guitarist's twang
Newly picked flowers
Demonica hated them all

What the mermaid sang
In those moonlit hours
Demonica hated it all

Earliest hints of Spring
In the swallow's song
Demonica hated it all

Ding-a-ling-a-ling
Ding-dong ding-dong
Demonica hated it all

Three wishes made
For what they're worth
Demonica hated them all

The rhythm of a spade
Digging clumps of earth
Demonica hated it all

A galloping horse
Across a galloping plain
Demonica hated it all

Wild bluebell gorse
In the wildwood rain
Demonica hated it all

A dance to be had
A trumpet to toot
Demonica hated it all

A chance to be glad
And a laugh and a hoot
Demonica hated it all

What the good life craves
When taking stock
Demonica hated it all

Those potato caves
Around Cuckoo Rock
Demonica hated them all.

WHAT DON, DEN AND DOUG SAID TO BILLY AND BOBBY

Don said 'done'

Den said 'then'

Doug said 'dig

Again and again'

Bobby said 'worry'

Billy said 'curse'

Don said 'hurry

Before it gets worse'

Billy said 'how?'

Bobby said 'when?'

Doug said 'now

Again and again'

Then:

White eyes white eyes
Never go black

White eyes white eyes
Coming back

Make a green thread
Spin it blue

Dig a pipeline
Through and through

Through to the wilderness
Through to the murk

White eyes white eyes
Watch us work

MAKE ME THIS

Make me rise, said Jasper.
Make me lift, said Don.
Make me pies, said Ivy.
Make me shift, said Stan.

Make me scream, said Demonica.
Make me bring, said Den.
Make me dream, said Gatherer.
Make me sting, said Fern.

Make me moss, said Ogre,
Make me lost so I forget.
Make me frost, said Julie.
Make me fast, said Jet.

Make me bow, said Morwenna,
Make me a part so I can sing.
Make me miaow said Woof.
Make me smart said Sting.

Make me jig, said Freaky.
Make me emerald, said Jade.
Make me dig, said Doug
To see what I have made.

WHAT IT ALL SAYS

Cuckoo Rock says: The Valley's magic.
The Valley says: It must not cease.
The nettles say: Make us ferns.
The plants whisper: Peace.

Ogre Rock says: Sand spoils darkness.
Demonica says: Rust never dies.
Moonlight says: Look at my shadow.
Sunset says: Look in my eyes.

The ghosts say: You can't see us.
Splatfish say: We only go 'splat!'
The stones say: A bridge over water.
The Cuckoo Man says: I'll dance to that.

The swallow says: Bring back tomorrow.
Tomorrow says: Time won't unlock.
The Yaffling Tree says: Where is the raven?
The raven says: At Cuckoo Rock.

THE MAGIC THREAD

The thread started small
But it had begun,
The work was cast,
The spell been spun,

The thread then spread —
Started creeping,
Spread as far
As where Demonica was sleeping,

It wrapped her up,
Took her out —
She couldn't scream
She couldn't shout,

She couldn't scare,
Couldn't shock —
It took her Over There
Away from Cuckoo Rock,

She couldn't spook
Couldn't be freaky —
So Goodness came back
Along with Mister Beaky —

The Yaffling Tree sang
As the Ogre Rock had left the hill
To the singing nettles and bracken
By the stream at Tinner's Mill.

HAPPY VALLEY

Demonica was blown away to Somewhere Else.

The valley would be good and not get bad.

The Night Soil Men dug.

The moonlight shone.

In Ivybridge a time could be had.

The Ogre Rock was crumbling into sand.

The valley would be good and not be bad.

The Night Soil Men worked.

The sonata ticked.

In Cuckootown — a time could be had.

The forces of disaster had gone away.

Dreams gathered in a time to be had.

The ghosts had taken fright.

The sunlight said goodnight.

The valley would be good and not get bad.

AS FAR AS WE COULD

We were feeling neither happy nor sad inside,
We'd been as far as we could on a magical ride,
The Dream Gatherer and I came to the edge of the lake,
We didn't know which path to take,
So we sat on the bank beneath the stars
And thought the whole wide world had now become ours.

We were feeling neither happy nor sad inside,
We'd been as far as we could on a magical ride,
I drank from the coolest water and she did too,
A feeling I'd not known before but somehow knew
And we both rose later on the dot of time,
Inside the sun was a reason, in the moon a rhyme.

We were feeling neither happy nor sad inside,
We'd been as far as we could on a magical ride,
We greeted the morning with the best of our hearts
Then took off on different ways from different starts,
But I still remember the water that both of us drank,
That path we didn't take, the one I have to thank.

GOOD SIGNS

Some say: go to the mountain,
Others: the path by the lake,
Some point you the way to the fountain.
Does it matter which one we take?

Some say: trust your own instincts,
Others: the song of the swallow,
Some say as far as the crow flies.
Which one do you think we should follow?

Some say: you always will find them,
Others: perhaps you may not,
But most say keep your eyes open.
Are they all so difficult to spot?

Yes!

As hard to find as the finger sign
On the hand of the talking clock
Crossing over the Clapper Bridge,
Heading for Cuckoo Rock.

Crossing over the Clapper Bridge
Heading for Cuckoo Rock.